Mysterious Monsters

Searching for Bigfoot

Jennifer Rivkin

PowerKiDS
press
New York

Published in 2015 by The Rosen Publishing Group, Inc.
29 East 21st Street, New York, NY 10010

Produced for Rosen by BlueApple*Works* Inc.
Art Director: Tibor Choleva
Designer: Joshua Avramson
Photo Research: Jane Reid
Editor for BlueApple*Works*: Melissa McClellan
US Editor: Joshua Shadowens

Illustrations: Cover, p. 1 T. Choleva; p. 4 Carlyn Iverson; p. 7 left dalmingo/Shutterstock

Photo Credits: Cover back, p. 1 BMJ/Shutterstock; p. 6 top Robert Crum/Dreamstime; p. 6, 12, 14, 15, 20 Fortean Picture Library; p. 6–7 bottom Dmitri Kotchetov/Dreamstime; p. 7 right Sergei Bachlakov/Dreamstime; p. 8 top Jane Rix/ Shutterstock; p. 8 Everett Collection/Shutterstock; p. 9, 10 top, 13 right, 19 right, 27, T. Choleva; p. 10 M. Niebuhr/ Shutterstock; p. 10–11 bottom Coronaandlime4me33/Dreamstime; p. 11 KEYSTONE Press; p. 12 top Maxim Khytra/ Shutterstock; p. 13 Jrockar/Dreamstime; p. 14 top Snehit/Shutterstock; p. 14 -15 background Brandon Bourdages/ Shutterstock; p. 16 top topten22photo/Shutterstock; p.16-17 background PhotoSky/Shutterstock; p. 17 sergioboccardo/ Shutterstock; p. 18 top Galyna Andrushko/Shutterstock; p. 18 M. McClellan; p. 19 left Steve Allen/Shutterstock; p. 20 top Pikoso.kz/Shutterstock; p. 21 Steve Busti; p/ 22 top Chris Hill/Shutterstock; p. 22 Ferenc Szelepcsenyi/Shutterstock; p. 23 jps/Shutterstock; p. 24 top Sergieiev/Shutterstock; p. 24 right Daderot/wikicommons; p.24 front right AVAVA/Shutterstock; p. 25 T.Choleva/AlessandroZocc/Shuttestock; p. 26 top Daniel Prudek/Shutterstock; p. 26 Marcio Silva/Dreamstime; p. 26–27 background Dmitry Pichugin/Dreamstime; p. 28 top James Wheeler/Shutterstock; p. 28 Blend Images/ Shutterstock; p. 28–29 background Robert Crum/Dreamstime; p. 29 Russell Linton/Dreamstime; paper background Fedorov Oleksiy/Shutterstock

Library of Congress Cataloging-in-Publication Data

Rivkin, Jennifer, author.
Searching for Bigfoot / by Jennifer Rivkin.
    pages cm. — (Mysterious monsters)
Includes index.
ISBN 978-1-4777-7105-1 (library binding) — ISBN 978-1-4777-7106-8 (pbk.) —
ISBN 978-1-4777-7107-5 (6-pack)
1. Sasquatch—Juvenile literature. I. Title
. QL89.2.S2R58 2015
001.944—dc23

                              2014001265

Manufactured in the United States of America

CPSIA Compliance Information: Batch #WS14PK8 For Further Information contact: Rosen Publishing, New York, New York at 1-800-237-9932

TABLE OF CONTENTS

WHAT IS BIGFOOT?

If you camp or hike in the woods of North America, you're likely to see certain animals. You'll surely spot a chipmunk or squirrel if you look up into the trees long enough. Other animals prefer to stay out of sight, but if you go deep into a forest, you may see a moose, deer, or bear.

Did you know that beyond the more common forest creatures, another type of animal may be hiding in the woods? Just like a bear, it's large, it's hairy, and it would prompt a difficult choice: a) stop and stare, or b) run for your life. But this is no ordinary animal. It is a legendary monster named Bigfoot.

THE GIANT APEMAN

Over the years, thousands of people across North America have claimed to see a giant apelike creature in the woods. They call it Bigfoot and describe it as being covered in brown or reddish hair, standing over 7 feet (2.1 m) tall, and weighing up to 500 pounds (227 kg). You would think that an animal this large couldn't be easily missed! As the name hints, Bigfoot has enormous footprints—as large as 24 inches (61 cm) long and 8 inches (20 cm) wide.

Is the monster real, or are the many stories about it based on mistaken identity, **hoaxes**, or wild imaginations? Read on and see what you think.

WHERE BIGFOOT PROWLS

The Pacific Northwest is often thought of as "Bigfoot Country," as most sightings have been in the western states of Washington, Oregon, and California. But the beast has also been spotted in mountains and forests across North America, especially in areas with dense woods that are mostly **uninhabited** by people.

Some researchers **hypothesize** that the creatures might migrate down to California, while others say that they tend to stay in one place.

◀ Apparently the creature doesn't have a climate preference. It has been seen as far south and east as Florida. In the South, it is often called a Skunk Ape due to its horrible smell.

OH, CANADA!

In Canada (and some western states), Bigfoot goes by the name Sasquatch. It has been spotted in every Canadian province, although most sightings have been in British Columbia, on the country's west coast. This is not surprising, as the province shares a border with Washington State, where so many American sightings take place. There is no reason for Sasquatches to stay within invisible borders.

DID YOU KNOW?

Sasquatch was at the Vancouver Olympics. Sasquatch played a prominent role in the 2010 Winter Olympics in Vancouver as one of the mascots. A brown, furry, earmuff-wearing Sasquatch, nicknamed "Quatchi," was on many souvenirs, from hats to books.

▼ *The Quatchi mascot was very popular at the Vancouver 2010 Winter Olympics.*

Yukon

British Columbia

Washington

Oregon

Ohio

Kentucky

New Jersey

Pennsylvania

◀ *Bigfoot has even made appearances in more populated eastern states like New Jersey, Pennsylvania, and Ohio.*

California

Texas

Florida

THE MYSTERY BEGINS

Bigfoot tales are not new. Stories of a strange creature roaming the woods have been common in the **folklore** of Native American tribes for centuries.

Some communities believe that Bigfoot is part of another native tribe. Others consider it to be a shy animal that is scared of humans. Some tribes worship the creature, believing that it has supernatural abilities and is a guardian of the forest. There are also frightening tales. For some tribes, Bigfoot is a monster that attacks humans and steals children—a beast that causes terror to flow through your veins.

▶ *The physical descriptions of Bigfoot creatures from differing tribes are similar. Interestingly, myths from long ago describe a figure that is eerily similar to those of the most recent eyewitness accounts.*

EARLY SIGHTINGS

In the early 1900s, miners, prospectors, and loggers were working in forests along the West Coast. In 1924, prospector Albert Ostman **recounted** having been abducted and held captive by a Sasquatch. That same year, in Washington, prospector Fred Beck and four other men said they were attacked by "apemen." During the day, one of the workers saw a Sasquatch in the woods and shot at it. That night, the men awoke to the sound of large rocks being thrown at their cabin. They also heard noise on the roof. Beck claimed to have seen at least three Sasquatches throwing rocks.

▶ Prospectors are people who search remote areas for natural resources such as minerals and oil. In the early 1900s, most American prospectors searched for gold and silver deposits in small rivers and creeks.

9

MODERN SIGHTINGS

It wasn't until the 1950s that the name "Bigfoot" first gained popularity. In 1958, bulldozer operator Gerald Crew discovered large footprints while working on road construction in an isolated area of Bluff Creek, California. He asked a friend to cast the prints in plaster, and the story was published in the *Humboldt Times* newspaper. The *Humboldt Times* editor, Andrew Genzoli, used the name "Bigfoot" in the article. The story gained international attention, and the name stuck.

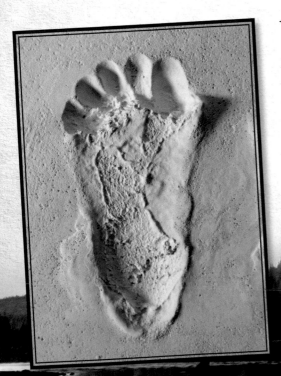

Years later, some claimed that the footprints had been a hoax staged by Ray Wallace, a local logger. Wallace was the brother of the man overseeing the construction work in Bluff Creek.

◄ *A plaster cast is made by pouring wet plaster into an indentation. When the plaster dries, people lift it out and keep it as evidence.*

Home Visits

There have been hundreds of Bigfoot sightings since then.

For example, in 1977, Barbara Sites claimed to have seen an 8-foot (2.4 m) Sasquatch with glowing red eyes on her family farm. She said that the animal had killed her rabbits and thrown her dog 20 feet (6 m).

In 2009, Kenny and Margaret Mahoney shot a picture of Bigfoot in their garden in Kentucky. They set up a motion camera after noticing that their homegrown vegetables were mysteriously disappearing. Expecting to capture images of a raccoon, they were shocked when the footage revealed a Sasquatch-type creature.

▶ *This is the photo of Bigfoot that Kenny and Margaret Mahoney shot in their back yard. Bigfoot has enough of a following to have attracted a team from the History Channel, who visited to Mahoneys to film an episode of their show MonsterQuest. With no Bigfoot spotted, the mystery continues.*

Lights, Camera, Action

In 1967, Bigfoot got another chance at fame when Roger Patterson and Robert Gimlin supposedly shot a short film of it in Bluff Creek, California. The duo had heard about the tracks there and went in search of Bigfoot. Patterson said that while riding horseback through the woods, he spotted the creature crouching beside a creek 50 feet (15 m) away. As the creature fled, Patterson started filming until he ran out of tape. He captured one minute of film—some of the ground, some of grainy images, and some of the creature.

◄ Patterson described Bigfoot as having a humanlike head with a large forehead and large nostrils. The animal's arms hung down to its knees. Long brown hair covered its entire body except its nose and mouth.

Was the Film a Flop?

The film caused a huge stir among Bigfoot hunters as well as the general public. Many believed it was **authentic** because it looked too real to be faked. The film showed a creature with long arms that was larger than a human and walked with knees bent. Viewers could even see muscles under the fur.

So, that's it then, right? The creature has been captured on film. It's real. The end. Well, not so fast. Most people now believe that the film was a hoax—a man in an ape suit. The footage was very unclear. The length of the steps in the film didn't match the footprints found there later.

Still, the movie has never been proven to be a hoax, and both men have always denied that they were part of one.

◄ Gorilla Run is a yearly event in many countries that raises awareness of the remaining 800 mountain gorillas in the wild. This charity run raises money to help save the species. Once the runners finish the race, they get to keep the gorilla suit. What would stop them from running for fun in local forests?

Bigfoot's Footprints

Since there is no "solid" proof of Bigfoot's existence, such as a body, bones, or a captured Bigfoot, footprints have been one of the main sources of **evidence** for believers. The prints found by Crew in Bluff Creek turned out to be a hoax, but thousands of others have been found since then. Many other people have made plaster casts of Bigfoot prints.

▲ Roger Patterson holds casts made from the footprints left in the ground at Bluff Creek after making the Bigfoot film.

STRANGE FOOT SHAPES

An average Bigfoot print is just over 16 inches (41 cm) long—the same length as basketball player Shaquille O'Neill's shoes. But the Bigfoot prints differ from Shaq's, and those of other humans, in several ways. The heels are larger, and the toes are of equal length. Many prints also show a midfoot pressure ridge. This feature is caused by the foot bending in the middle before taking the next step. Most human feet do not have this feature, but many apes do.

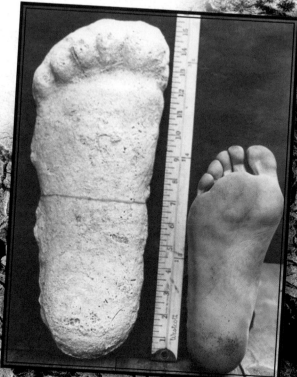

▶ A human foot is compared for size with the cast of a Bigfoot print. Scientists also take note of the space between footprints. Often, they are over 3 feet (0.9 m) apart, suggesting that a very tall animal made them.

SCIENCE AND RESEARCH

While some eyewitnesses are caught off guard by seeing a strange creature in the woods, others have formed groups to find it. The most notable one is the Bigfoot Field Researchers Organization (BFRO). Founded in 1995 by Matt Moneymaker, the group is made up of scientists, journalists, and others who conduct research in the field as well as in laboratories. BFRO sends teams to places where sightings have occurred to collect physical evidence. The group's goal is to solve the mystery once and for all.

▲ Even nonmembers over 21 years of age can take part in these four-day excursions around the United States and Canada. BFRO's website features a database that is updated with the most recent Bigfoot sightings from across North America.

THE SCIENCE OF BIGFOOT

DNA analysis has become an important scientific tool for Bigfoot researchers. DNA from an unknown animal can be compared to the code from known animals. Scientists can determine the type of animal by testing DNA from hair, bones, or blood.

In 2013, after a five-year study of Bigfoot DNA samples, Dr. Melba Ketchum and a team of researchers announced that they had found evidence of Bigfoot. The team reported that, over the years, they had collected and studied 113 samples of hair, blood, toenails, and tissue thought to belong to a Sasquatch (Bigfoot). The samples turned out to be human, but some of the DNA belonged to an unknown **species**. Members of the "Sasquatch Genome Project" claim that Bigfoot is an ancient **hybrid** cross between a human and another **primate**. However, no serious scientific journal thought the study worthy of publishing.

▶ *In 2005, a group of people in Yukon, Canada, spotted a Bigfoot-type creature and gathered a tuft of its hair. They sent it to a scientist at the University of Alberta. Dr. David Coltman tested the sample and found that it came from a bison, proving that the hair was a hoax.*

BIGFOOT UP-CLOSE

If you're going into the woods anytime soon, you may want to know what to look or listen for when searching for Bigfoot. You may hear a Bigfoot before you see it. Bigfoot enthusiasts say that the creatures throw rocks or bang sticks on trees. They also screech, moan, and howl.

You may see and hear a Bigfoot coming, but did you also know that you might smell one? Bigfoot is said to carry a strong odor that has been described as a mixture of **feces** and rotting meat. According to BFRO, about 10 to 15 percent of people who claim to have seen the creature have also noted a smell.

◀ Do the creatures make themselves stink, or are they trying to hide their own scent? Dogs are known to roll around in feces. This behavior is both common and natural. Long ago, dogs' wild ancestors masked their scent so they could sneak up on prey. Wolves have been observed masking their scent before a hunt by rolling in animal droppings or carcasses.

Home, Sweet Home

According to some BFRO researchers, Bigfoot might sleep in large nests on the ground. In 2001, Kathy Moskowitz Strain, an **anthropologist** and forest worker, found a site with three possible Bigfoot "nests" in Sonora, California. One of these domed structures measured 4.3 feet (1.3 m) high, 5.2 feet (1.6 m) wide, and 6.2 feet (1.9 m) long. Made of oak and pine, the inside had soft padding made of moss, ferns, and oak leaves. Moskowitz noted an imprint, possibly from a large body, in the nest. She also found Bigfoot tracks nearby.

Eyewitness Tale

Truthfully, this one's more of an earwitness tale. In 1984, Bruce Hoffman was prospecting for gold near the Clackamas River in Oregon. He later told people that he heard a yell from far off in the woods. The loud sound shocked him, as he had never heard anything like it before—not from a human nor from any other animal. Others have described hearing screeches and moans coming from the woods.

◀ *Other researchers suggest that Bigfoot lives in caves, so you may want to be extra careful when hiking through an area with these built-in hiding places.*

HOAXES AND FAKES

Whether to be part of history or because they enjoy playing pranks, **tricksters** have had great fun with Bigfoot folklore. Many people have worn ape costumes, and some have gone to even greater lengths to pull off a hoax.

As mentioned earlier, some of the first reported Bigfoot sightings are now considered hoaxes. There's the alleged prank by Ray Wallace that ended up as a story in the *Humboldt Times*, the Patterson-Gimlin film, and Cripplefoot. One of the men who "found" the print was a known hoaxster.

◄ *Bigfoot was supposedly photographed by a forest patrol officer at Wild Creek, Washington, in 1995. The photograph was eventually declared to be a hoax.*

THE MINNESOTA ICEMAN

One of the most famous hoaxes was the Minnesota Iceman, supposedly a Bigfoot-type creature frozen in ice. Sideshow exhibitor Frank Hansen toured carnivals, fairs, and shopping malls with the exhibit during the 1960s and 1970s. In 1968, researchers said that the Iceman was real and a new species of Neanderthal, an early human. They even published the findings in a scientific journal. Later, the Smithsonian Institution determined that the "creature" was made of latex rubber.

▲ Steve Busti, the owner of the Museum of the Weird in Texas, stands in front of the Minnesota Iceman display. The detailed image on the right shows the face and the chest of the "Iceman."

Scientific View

Most scientists believe that Bigfoot isn't real, and not because they don't want it to be. In fact, Jane Goodall, a famous **primatologist**, has been quoted as saying she would love for the creatures to exist.

Scientists point out that great apes do not live in the regions where Bigfoot has been sighted. Just as important, hundreds if not thousands of people have searched for the creature over the years, and no one has ever found a body, bones, or teeth. No one has managed to capture a Bigfoot or get a clear video, either. The high number of hoaxes make scientists even more **skeptical**.

◀ Jane Goodall is considered the foremost expert on chimpanzees in the world. Goodall is best known for her decades-long study of wild chimpanzee behavior in Gombe Stream National Park, Tanzania.

What About the Sightings?

Not all eyewitnesses are lying. Scientists think that most are probably making an honest mistake. They may be seeing a bear standing on its hind legs and be confusing it with a Bigfoot. If they believe that creatures live in the woods and expect (or want) to see one, their minds may play tricks on them.

Eyewitnesses may also be seeing someone wearing a ghillie suit, a type of camouflage clothing worn by hunters, soldiers, and nature photographers. The suit is made from strips of burlap, cloth, or twine and is made to look like leaves, vines, and twigs. The purpose is to make the wearer blend in with the forest.

▶ A ghillie suit is meant to resemble dense plants. There have been several reports of people in ghillie suits trying to pull a Bigfoot prank. Unfortunately, not all pranks are harmless. According to CNN, one such prankster was killed in a car accident in 2012 while crossing a forest highway.

WHO COULD BIGFOOT BE?

One theory is that Bigfoot might be a descendant of Neanderthals. Another is that Bigfoot is an ancient ape descended from a prehistoric primate called *Gigantopithecus blacki*. Millions of years ago, *Gigantopithecus* lived in what is now Asia. Supporters of this theory suggest that the ape crossed the Bering land bridge between Asia and North America thousands of years ago and that its ancestors are still living in the United States and Canada.

▶ Gigantopithecus blacki *was huge, as its name suggests. It may have been 10 feet (3 m) tall and weighed 500 pounds (227 kg). The tallest professional basketball player in the world, Paul Sturgess, is "only" 7 feet 7.26 inches (2.318 m) tall.*

THE THEORIES EXPLORED

Some scientists say that *Gigantopithecus blacki* was too big to walk on two feet. But since full fossil remains have never been found, only part of a jawbone, they can't be certain. Is it possible that *Gigantopithecus blacki* did not face extinction years ago as previously thought? It's a long shot, but…maybe.

Formerly unknown animals are found every year. In 2007, scientists found a new primate, a lesula monkey, in the Democratic Republic of the Congo. The species had never before been classified by scientists. Other animals, including the megamouth shark, giant squid, and Komodo dragon, were considered legends until they were found.

◀ *Species previously thought to be extinct have been found. For example, the coelacanth, a fish believed to have gone extinct about 66 million years ago, was found in 1937 off the coast of South Africa.*

BIGFOOT'S COUSINS?

North Americans aren't the only people who have seen large apelike creatures roaming the woods. Sightings of Bigfoot-type animals have been noted on every continent except Antarctica. There's the Yowie in Australia, the Xucren of China, and the Hibagon of Japan, to name just a few.

Another, the Orang Pendek, is said to live in the rainforests of Sumatra. Just like Bigfoot, first natives and later colonists claimed to have seen it. But scientists have been unable to prove that it exists. They say that eyewitnesses may have mistaken local animals for the Orang Pendek.

◄ *In Russia, stories of a large apelike creature named the Alma go back for centuries. Almas are said to look more like hairy humans than apes. Witnesses described Almas as about 6 feet (1.8 m) tall with flat noses, weak chins, large eyebrows, and bodies covered with reddish-brown hair.*

THE ABOMINABLE SNOWMAN

The Himalayas are a vast mountain range that runs through northern India, Nepal, Bhutan, Tibet, and China. They are over 1,500 miles (2,414 km) long and 100 miles (161 km) wide. The Himalayas are home to some of the world's tallest peaks, including Mount Everest. They may also be home to a creature quite similar to Bigfoot. Abominable Snowman (or Yeti) sightings have been reported for centuries. Many local cultures worship the creatures, while others fear it. Either way, they all agree that Yeti exists.

▶ Scientists have examined some of the "evidence" that Yetis exist and have concluded that it is from other animals. However, the creature may be lurking in an unexplored part of the Himalayas. If there are only a small number of Yetis, and if they only hunt at night, they would be very hard to discover.

What Do You Think?

Is it just a **coincidence** that most Native American tribes have a Bigfoot-type creature as part of their mythology? Moreover, could it be mere coincidence that the folklore of people on every continent describes animals so similar? The native stories were told before people across continents could communicate easily. Maybe something in human nature makes us believe—or want to believe—in a creature so similar yet different from us. It is also possible that such a creature really does exist.

◀ *The next time you go hiking with your family through North American wilderness, pay close attention to your surroundings. Watch for unusual sights and sounds. And, of course, have your camera ready! It might be you who will solve the mystery of Bigfoot by snapping a clear picture of the creature.*

Hairy and Famous

Bigfoot is one of the most famous monsters in the world. In early 2014, a new show on Spike TV called *10 Million Dollar Bigfoot Bounty* premiered. Contestants hunt Bigfoot and must come up with real proof to win the big prize. Should Lloyd's of London, the company that would be forking over the prize money, be worried? What do you think?

It seems that interest in the creature will not die down, no matter what evidence scientists have to offer. After all, while so much land is still unexplored, who knows what they—or you—will find?

▶ *If you ever go to Pikes Peak, which is 10 miles (16 km) west of Colorado Springs, Colorado, be sure to look for Bigfoot. There have been so many sightings on the way up that officials put up a warning sign where sightings are most common.*

BIG FOOT XING

DUE TO SIGHTINGS IN THE AREA OF A CREATURE RESEMBLING "BIG FOOT" THIS SIGN HAS BEEN POSTED FOR YOUR SAFETY

GLOSSARY

anthropologist (an-thruh-PAH-luh-jist) A scientist who studies humans, including their origins, characteristics, and culture.

authentic (ah-THEN-tik) Real; true and accurate.

coincidence (koo-IN-suh-dents) Something that can only be explained by chance or luck.

DNA (DEE IN AY) A substance that carries genetic information in the cells of plants and animals.

evidence (EH-vuh-dunts) Facts which prove or disprove that something exists.

feces (FEE-seez) Solid waste that is released from the body.

folklore (FOHK-lor) Beliefs and stories handed down from generation to generation.

hoaxes (HOHKS-ez) Acts meant to trick people into believing or accepting as genuine things that are false and often preposterous.

hybrid (HY-brud) An animal or plant that is produced from two animals or plants of different kinds.

hypothesize (hy-PAH-theh-syz) To suggest (an idea or theory).

primate (PRY-mayt) Any member of the group of animals that includes human beings, apes, and monkeys.

primatologist (pry-muh-TAH-luh-jist) A person who studies primates, especially those other than modern humans.

recounted (rih-KOWN-ted) Told in detail.

skeptical (SKEP-ti-kul) Having or expressing doubt, either in general or about a certain statement or topic.

species (SPEE-sheez) A category of living things that are similar to each other and are able to produce offspring.

tricksters (TRIK-stirs) Dishonest people who try to fool others.

uninhabited (un-in-HA-but-ed) Not settled or lived in by people.

FOR MORE INFORMATION

FURTHER READING

Hawkins, John. *Bigfoot and Other Monsters*. Mystery Hunters. New York: PowerKids Press, 2012.

Roberts, Steven. *Bigfoot!* Jr. Graphic Monster Stories. New York: PowerKids Press, 2012.

Troupe, Thomas Kingsley. *The Legend of Bigfoot*. Legend Has It. Mankato, MN: Capstone Press, 2011.

WEBSITES

Due to the changing nature of Internet links, PowerKids Press has developed an online list of websites related to the subject of this book. This site is updated regularly. Please use this link to access the list:

www.powerkidslinks.com/mymo/bfoot/

INDEX